THE GIFT
OF THE
VIOLET FLAME

THE GIFT
OF THE
VIOLET FLAME

An Easy Way to Teach Spirituality
to Your Family

ELIZABETH CLARE PROPHET

SUMMIT UNIVERSITY PRESS®

Gardiner, Montana

THE GIFT OF THE VIOLET FLAME:
An Easy Way to Teach Spirituality to Your Family
Elizabeth Clare Prophet

For information:
The Summit Lighthouse, 63 Summit Way, Gardiner, MT 59030 USA
1-800-245-5445 / 406-848-9500
TSLinfo@TSL.org
SummitLighthouse.org

Library of Congress Control Number: 2017961402
ISBN: 978-1-60988-283-9 (eBook)
ISBN: 978-1-60988-284-6 (softbound)

SUMMIT UNIVERSITY 🔥 PRESS®

Summit University Press, 🔥, The Summit Lighthouse, 🔥 and *Pearls of Wisdom* are trademarks registered in the U.S. Patent and Trademark Office and in other countries. All rights to their use are reserved.

Disclaimer: Results from the practices recommended in this book may vary depending on individual circumstances. This book is for informational purposes only and is not a replacement for advice from licensed professionals in the fields of family counseling, social work, health, psychology, education, finance or law.

CONTENTS

To Parents, Teachers, and Friends of the Child,

Welcome to the joyful journey of learning about the wonders of the violet flame! We hope that you and your family will enjoy your time together as you discover the many practical teachings and exciting activities included in this book for families—*The Gift of the Violet Flame*.

Profound Teachings and Fun Activities

These profound teachings and activities are conveyed in a way that makes learning about the violet flame a fun and memorable experience for children. As you read the inspiring and lighthearted wisdom found within the pages of this book, you will find many select teachings given by Mark and Elizabeth Clare Prophet that are relevant for raising children. These teachings have been compiled by the editors of Summit University Press with the helpful guidance of parents and teachers.

Children will learn how the many graces of the violet flame can bring great joy into their lives, improve their relationships, and help them have a deeper connection with God in their hearts. They will learn how the violet flame can help solve specific problems and how they can use the violet flame to help others, including those in their communities and in the world.

There are several engaging hands-on activities included in each chapter that you and your family can enjoy doing together. For example, children can create a violet-flame snow globe, learn about the violet flame while using sidewalk chalk, and make delightful violet-flame goo! They will also learn how to give violet-flame mantras and decrees and how to set up their own altar for their prayer and devotional time.

How to Adapt this Book for Children of All Ages

This book is most suitable for children ages four through ten, although it can be easily adapted for younger or older children. We recommend that you, as parent, teacher, or friend of the child, read each chapter to your child rather than having your child read it on their own. Or you and your child can take turns reading. The goal is to make the experience a special and interactive one for all.

We also suggest that you review each chapter before presenting it to your child. This will allow you to assimilate the teaching and to adapt it to the child's specific age and needs. For example, you may want to change some of the wording to fit what you know is going on in your child's life. This will help make the teaching more meaningful to him or her, which is of course how a young person learns best!

Have Fun Learning Together!

Research shows that parents are ultimately the best teachers for their children, especially when it comes to guiding them in their spiritual lives. Other family members, teachers and friends also have a great influence on the child. This book is intended to assist children in learning about the violet flame with the most important people in their lives. So have fun together!

If you are new to the teachings on the violet flame, you can have a great time learning right along with your child. And even if you've known about the violet flame for a while, it is very likely that you will learn new things about it as you read this book!

As the whole family gets involved in learning about the violet flame, all may experience the many blessings that this special light can bring, such as deeper spirituality, closer family ties, positive changes, and greater joy.

Discovering Teachable Moments

The more you become familiar with these magnificent teachings on the violet flame, the more you will find "teachable moments" that naturally occur with your child throughout the day. If you are in a park, for example, you might talk with your child about how the violet flame can help the nature spirits. Or if your child is telling you about a difficult situation he or she is facing with someone at school, you might talk about how the violet flame can help resolve such challenges. The more you absorb the teachings of the violet flame, the more these precious moments can occur.

We wish you and your family a most wondrous journey as you have fun learning about the violet flame together and making it a part of your life!

The Editors of Summit University Press®

CHAPTER ONE

Sparkle and Shine with the Violet Flame!

"One of the first feelings you will have when you use the violet flame is the feeling of joy. The joyousness of freedom and the buoyant feeling of release come with that flame. When you are bathed with the violet flame, you want to sing and dance and flow with life. It is a new freedom."

Elizabeth Clare Prophet, March 23, 1974

The Gift of the Violet Flame

Imagine that one fine morning a dear friend hands you a package. It is wrapped in sparkling violet-colored paper and tied with a deep purple ribbon. You shake it, but nothing rattles. What is it? You simply can't wait to open it! Your friend explains that this is one of the greatest gifts of all and that this gift has been given by spiritual teachers to their students for thousands of years. The gift is free. The gift is powerful. But if you don't invite it into your life, it can do nothing for you. The gift has remained a veiled secret to many upon the planet. For mysterious reasons, it's your turn to receive this stupendous gift.

Suddenly, violet light shoots out of the package and dances on the wall like lively flames. You gasp. It's stunning! The gift seems to reach out to you! Now what? Your friend explains that you will have to learn how to use this gift and that it will take some time to completely understand it. Your friend then whispers two sacred words in your ear: "Violet flame!" You are surprised to hear these words and wonder, "What is the violet flame?"

You may also wonder why the violet flame is one of the greatest gifts of all. Well, this is because it's the flame of freedom! The violet flame can do many things for you, but most importantly it can free you to have a greater connection to God in your heart. With the violet flame you can be free to be who you really are. You can do what you are meant to do. Wow! You can become a better son or daughter, a better sister or brother, a better friend. It can also help you solve daily challenges of all kinds. We all have challenges, great and small. The violet flame can help you conquer yours. It can make a huge difference in your life. You might not know it now, but the violet flame is one of the best gifts you will ever receive. What you do with this gift is up to you!

The Violet Flame Is a Spiritual Light

The violet flame is a beautiful and uplifting light that affects both the physical and spiritual worlds. The physical world is anything we can experience with our five senses, which are sight, sound, smell, taste, and touch. The spiritual world is that which we can't see with our eyes or experience with our other senses. Sometimes people who close their eyes and meditate on the love of God in their hearts can "see" the violet flame at a spiritual level. Some saints and mystics have reported the inner experience of seeing a violet light during prayer and meditation.

We all experience the blessings and gifts of the violet flame once in a while, whether we know it or not. You might remember times in your life when you felt very joyful and peaceful inside, your heart full and warm. You may have felt full of happiness and excitement about life. Maybe you even felt inspired with all kinds of creative ideas. It's likely you had no worries at all and felt that all was right with the world. At times like these, you can be sure that the violet flame—this special light of God—was there! Can you think of times when you felt like this?

Even though most people don't know about the violet flame, many people feel its presence when they have these feelings of joy and lightness in their heart. People sense this energy. It feels light and free. Do you know what it means when we talk about energy? You will probably realize what it means when you hear more about it.

We Feel All Kinds of Energy

Energy is something you've probably felt, even if you've never thought about it before. It's that subtle feeling you may have as you go from place to place. Energy can be positive or it can be negative. It can feel good or it can feel bad. For example, have you ever walked into a church or other place of worship where people are quietly praying and you noticed how beautiful and peaceful it felt? This is positive energy. It feels light and uplifting. You might also feel positive energy when you're in nature, like when you're walking on a quiet trail or sitting by a dazzling waterfall. You feel peaceful and calm in these places.

On the other hand, there is negative energy. What do we mean by that? Have you ever walked into a room that was dusty and disorganized, with a heavy feeling in the air? Maybe it's a place or a room where people don't go very often. It might even feel a little creepy. That's an example of negative energy. Or have you ever been on a crowded city sidewalk where people are in a hurry and maybe a bit grumpy? Do you feel like getting away from this negative energy? Most people do! The violet flame can help you in situations like this because it changes negative energy into positive energy. You will soon learn more about how this happens.

The Violet Flame Is Easy to Use

You might feel that you have so many things to do, like homework, chores, or band practice, that you don't have time to learn about the violet flame or to use it. Here is a secret: The violet flame is easy to use! It can help you do everything on your list—and everything in your life. Because the violet flame changes negative energy into positive energy, your chores will be easier! When you have that light and cheerful feeling, everything becomes more fun, right? Maybe your room won't magically clean itself, but you can feel more lighthearted while you clean it! You can bring the violet flame into your world, and you can also send it to others so that it helps them too. It can help if you've had a disagreement with a friend or someone you love, and it can help if someone has hurt your feelings. It sounds pretty wonderful, doesn't it?

All You Have to Do Is Ask!

Now you've learned about the gift of the violet flame. Are you sitting on the edge of your seat waiting to learn how to use it? First, it's good to remember that we have the light of God in our hearts. The more of this light we have, the more joy and peace we feel. So, what do we do when we need something from God? We ask! Yes, all we have to do is ask God for it! Your prayer can be as simple as, "Dear God, please send violet flame into this situation now!" And there it is!

Now, as you give your prayer, or mantra, for the violet flame to come into your life, there's one more little secret you should know about your violet-flame gift. Do you have any idea why the violet flame works so well? Well, there are special blessings that come into your life when you ask for the violet flame. Two of these blessings are mercy and forgiveness. So when you pray for the violet flame to help you, these very qualities are helping to change negative situations into positive ones. Isn't that amazing? Do you think it's worth a try?

---- **FUN FAMILY ACTIVITIES** ----

ACTIVITY #1:
Poof! Goes the Violet Flame

Goal: The goal of this activity is to demonstrate how the violet flame can help clear away problems and negative energy quickly.

Materials:
> A large, clear glass bowl
> Black pepper in a shaker so it can be sprinkled easily
> Purple liquid dish soap
> (If you can't find purple dish soap, you can add a little blue and
>   red food coloring to white or clear dish soap.)

Preparation: Fill the bowl with water. Have the black pepper and dish soap close by.

The Activity: Explain to the children that the black pepper represents negative energy, which can sometimes be feelings of fear, anger, discouragement, etc. Ask each child to sprinkle some black pepper into the bowl of water. Make sure they sprinkle enough pepper so it can be seen floating on the surface of the water. Then explain that the violet flame helps negative energy go away. Demonstrate this by taking the dish soap and squeezing a drop into the water, right onto the black pepper.

What happens next is quick and dramatic. The purple dish soap makes the black pepper shoot to the sides of the bowl. Poof! There goes the negative energy! This action represents the violet flame taking away negativity, or darkness, so that light and good things can come.

ACTIVITY #2:
From Dull to Dazzling

Goal: The goal of this experiment is to demonstrate how the violet flame can clean up negative energy.

Materials:
> A few dull, old pennies
> ¼ cup of white vinegar
> Violet or purple watercolor paint
> Small paintbrush
> 1 teaspoon of salt
> Non-metal bowl
> Paper towels

Preparation: Collect the materials. Pour the white vinegar into the bowl and stir in the salt. Add the paint and stir to make a pretty shade of violet.

The Activity: Ask the children to describe the pennies. They will probably notice that the pennies are dull and dirty. Then explain that the solution in the bowl represents the violet flame. Ask the children what they think the violet flame does. Put several pennies into the violet solution. Have everyone count slowly and dramatically to ten. Make it exciting! Now take the pennies out of the bowl and rinse them off in water. Hold them up so all can see that the pennies are now bright and shiny. This is the effect that the violet flame can have on everything. It can make anything sparkle and shine!

ACTIVITY #3:
Violet-Flame Nature Walk

Goal: The goal of this simple family activity is to observe the many ways that the beautiful color violet appears in nature.

Materials: None

Preparation: In spring or summer, research local trails where wildflowers or many types of rocks and minerals might be seen. This can be a family activity, when everyone decides together where to go on the walk. Pack your backpacks and water bottles, and off you go!

The Activity: When the weather is good, take your violet-flame nature walk on your chosen trail. Look for violet flowers or other things along the way, even rocks or crystals that have a violet hue. This is a fun activity, especially for young children. You might all be surprised at how much the color violet appears in nature all around us. Some children might enjoy making a list of their violet-colored discoveries. Others might like taking photos that can be printed and put into a violet-flame book. Use your creativity to take note of the beautiful violet colors that you see, or ask your children for their ideas!

CHAPTER TWO

The Light Rays of God

*"The time for mankind's realization and application of
this flame has come.... How does your soul get to God?
By your invocation of this flame."*

Elizabeth Clare Prophet, *Inner Perspectives*

Everyone Loves Rainbows!

Have you ever seen a rainbow after a refreshing summer storm, with its dazzling array of colors? Everyone loves rainbows! How do you feel when you look at one? Most people have a sense of wonder when they see this beautiful display of nature. The violet band of the rainbow seems to magically melt right into the sky above you, fading into the infinite reaches of space. It seems to connect earth with heaven.

When you look at a rainbow, you will see how the beautiful violet color looks as if there were more to the rainbow than the physical eye can see. This is because the violet light has the highest frequency of visible light. The violet light is right at the point of change from the visible world to the invisible world. This is also the point between the physical world and the spiritual world. To some people, even as far back as in ancient times, this transitional and transcendent color was a spiritual wonder.

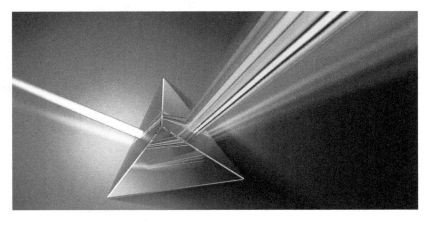

There is another way you can see rainbows, and that is right in your very own home. If you take a prism, which is a type of crystal, and hold it up to the sunlight, you will see beautiful little rainbows dancing around on the walls or ceiling. This happens because the white light of the sun hits the prism and then separates into the seven colors of the rainbow. These colors are red, orange, yellow, green, blue, indigo, and violet.

God's Seven Rays of Light

Did you know that God loves you so much that he wants you to have his light so that you can be more like him? In the spiritual world there are seven rainbow rays that come out of the pure white light of God. He sends these light rays to you for the nourishing of your heart and soul. These glowing light rays from the heart of God also come in many magnificent colors, including the color violet.

You might recognize some of the qualities of the light rays of God in everyday life around you. For example, the blue ray represents God's will, strength, and protection. This may be why policemen often wear blue uniforms. The yellow ray represents wisdom and illumination. Sometimes this light of wisdom is shown as a halo of golden light around people who are very close to God. The pink ray is the flame of love, which is probably why we see pink hearts on Valentine's Day cards. The white ray focuses purity, which explains why many brides wear lovely white dresses. The green ray is the ray of healing and supply. You may notice that green is a color often associated with health and healing. The sixth ray of purple and gold represents ministration and service, which is the ray of helping people. And the violet ray, also called the seventh ray, is the ray of freedom.

The Many Shades of Violet

The colors violet and purple have been used throughout history to convey spirituality and royalty. You may have read stories with pictures of kings and queens wearing attractive purple robes. This is because purple, which is the deeper shade of violet, is a sign of nobility. These beautiful purple robes also protected the kings and queens from negative energy so they could do their job.

During the time that kings and queens wore their royal robes, there were often magnificent dances, called balls, where everyone waltzed to uplifting music. Can you imagine the ladies in their lovely, flowing dresses, many of them heavenly shades of pink, violet, and purple, as they twirled across the room?

They might have also worn blue, indigo, periwinkle, lavender, and all of the many hues of the violet spectrum of color. This must have been an amazing sight!

There is a reason why there are so many shades of violet, and it is because the violet flame has many qualities of God contained within it. You've already heard about the qualities of mercy and forgiveness. There are a few other qualities too, such as justice, tact, and diplomacy. (We'll talk more about these later.) God is very creative in how he expresses himself!

Violet-Flame Treasures

If you're like most kids, you're probably busy doing all kinds of fun things. You may be so busy that you might not think about the light of God all that much. Maybe it would be helpful if you had something to remind you about his light and of the light of the violet flame as you go about your day. Here are a few ideas:

There are sparkling violet crystals that you can find in stores, which carry the energy and light of the violet flame. One of these is the amethyst crystal. The amethyst can be worn as jewelry, or you can place an amethyst crystal on your desk or your special place of prayer. The color violet is also used in art and fashion. A nice violet sweater or stylish scarf can be quite the fashion statement! Violet is also frequently used in home décor, so it's fun to have a few decorative violet items around the house as a reminder of the beautiful gift of the violet flame!

A Mantra to the Violet Flame

You've learned so much about the violet flame already! Would you like to try a short mantra to help bring the violet flame into your heart and all around you? A mantra is a simple prayer, which you can say over and over again if you want to. And the more you give that mantra, the more light you will receive.

When you give a violet-flame mantra, the violet flame surrounds you like dancing, singing flames. You might not actually see the violet flame around you, but some people feel it, especially in their heart. Would you like to try a violet-flame mantra to see if you can feel it? But don't worry if you don't! Sometimes it takes practice.

God has taught us that we can ask for his light by saying his name, which he told to Moses a very long time ago. Do you know what God's name is? In the English language his name is "I AM THAT I AM."

You will see that the following mantra says the words "I AM." The "I AM" part of the mantra refers to the I AM THAT I AM. When you say "I AM," you are saying that "God in me is." You are accepting God's light into your heart. In the following mantra you are especially asking for the violet flame to come into your heart, your whole being, your whole world, and into any situation you would like it to go to.

You can say this mantra one time or as many times as you like.

I AM a being of violet fire!

I AM the purity God desires!

You can even use this mantra for your pets! You can put the name of your pet or pets in the blank and then give the mantra just like this:

[_____] is a being of violet fire!

[_____] is the purity God desires!

Try this mantra and notice how you feel when you are filled with the violet flame!

FUN FAMILY ACTIVITIES

ACTIVITY #1:
Rainbow-Rays Artwork

Goal: The goal of this activity is to see a rainbow from light rays shining through a crystal.

Materials:
    Multi-faceted crystals
    Plain white paper
    Colored pencils
    A sunny window where you can hold the crystals up to the sun

Preparation: Gather the materials and set them up near the sunny window.

The Activity: Hold the crystal up to the sunlight. Look for the rainbows that come through the crystal and can be seen on the walls, the floor, or wherever they appear. Then position the crystal so that the rainbow shines onto a piece of white paper. Family members can then color the rainbow on the paper to create their own rainbow-rays artwork.

ACTIVITY #2:
Rainbow Bubbles

Goal: The goal of this activity is to see the rainbows shimmering on the surface of bubbles. This is another way to see rainbows in a fun and interactive way.

Materials:
> A lovely sunny day
> Bubble solution
> Bubble-blowing wands
> An electric fan

Preparation: Gather the materials and go outside.

The Activity: Blow bubbles in the sun. The bubbles will be clear no matter what color the bubble solution is, but they will still shimmer with rainbow colors. If you would like your bubbles to go even higher into the sky, plug in the large fan and blow bubbles in front of it. Your bubbles might bring some joy to your neighbors as the bubbles gently float into their yards!

ACTIVITY #3:
A Gentle Summer Rainbow

Goal: The goal of this activity is to see a rainbow from the spray of water coming from a garden hose. This is a summer activity.

Materials:

An outside garden hose

Preparation: None

The Activity: On a hot, sunny summer day, go outside to a garden hose in the yard. Turn on the hose and hold it off the ground so the spray of water is in the sunlight. Look for the rainbow that appears in the spray of water as the sunshine hits it. Optional: Cool everyone off afterward with a gentle spray from the hose!

CHAPTER THREE

Fill Your Being with Light!

"The violet transmuting flame works. It really works....
If I was ever skeptical about the violet flame, I wasn't after
using it for six months—I'll tell you that."

Mark L. Prophet, *Violet Flame: Alchemy for Personal Change*

The Violet Flame Will Make You Free

Imagine that you are hiking along a mountain trail. The air is clean and crisp. You love looking up at the beautiful scenery, but you don't always watch your step. Occasionally you trip on some rocks and you stumble along the way. The rocks make the hike more challenging.

Life sometimes has bumps along the way, like those rocks along the hiking trail. Isn't it better to remove these obstacles than to have to walk around them? If you think about it, those rocks on our path are like karma. Have you ever heard of the word *karma* before? We can think of karma as situations in our life that are the result of something we did in this life or a previous life. (More on that later.) Karma appears in our life for balance and resolution and to teach us the lessons our soul needs in order to learn and grow. This, again, is where the violet flame can help us. Giving mantras to the violet flame can make those boulders of karma smaller, or even remove them completely. And you won't stub your toe as often on the path of life if you give the violet flame!

Feeling Stuck...

Sometimes emotions can come up when playing with friends or because of difficult situations at school. For example, maybe you have some interesting thoughts about a book your class is reading together. You would love to raise your hand and share those thoughts in a group discussion, but you feel afraid. You don't want anyone to laugh at you! Or maybe you found out that a friend of yours has been talking behind your back. You would love to talk to him or her about it, but you don't enjoy bringing up things that bother you. So instead, you keep your feelings to yourself and you end up feeling bottled up and resentful. Learning how to handle these deep feelings are a normal part of growing up, and the violet flame is a wonderful tool to help. You might think of these negative feelings as similar to molasses. They slow you down and sometimes make you feel like you can't take another step. This is really feeling stuck!

Getting Unstuck—
the Violet Flame Changes Darkness into Light!

You can probably think of a few "rocks" that get in your way and make you feel stuck sometimes. Wouldn't it be wonderful to get rid of those situations or feelings that hold you back? You might imagine the violet flame as a magic solvent, like a very special soap that goes into your every cell and cleans out all of the karmic debris that has collected there. (This includes your physical body as well as your thoughts, feelings, and memories.)

When you give your violet-flame mantras, you can name all of the situations and feelings that you would like to see cleared from your entire being. The violet flame can change, or transmute, the negative energy and emotions that come up in everyday situations. It can fill the spaces in each atom and cell with light. The violet flame doesn't just remove the debris; it transforms it into light! The violet flame can transmute feelings of fear and doubt into feelings of confidence. You feel free of obstacles that have kept you from being who you really are!

The Violet Flame Is Scientific

Do you have a favorite song or a piece of music that you love to listen to? We know that when we listen to a piece of music that we love, it has its own tone and melody that makes it sound just right. But if a friend tries to sing that song or play that music, it might not sound very good if your friend is off key. And don't we wish we could do something about that!

Everything on earth—from trees and flowers to the atoms and cells in our bodies—has its own vibration, its own tone.

Even *you* have your very own tone. We can also call this a key-note. When an object vibrates at its keynote, it is at its highest energy level. Now, here's some really good news! The violet flame helps everything get back to its original keynote. No wonder the violet flame helps us to be who we really are!

Since the violet flame is the spiritual flame that is closest in vibration to everything in our physical world, it affects physical matter. When the violet flame touches something, it "sings" the keynote of that object. The energy of that object then rises to that keynote. And most amazing of all, the violet flame sings as it *consumes* all that is out of tune with the original keynote of that object! In other words, the violet flame takes away the bad stuff and keeps the good stuff!

Try this experiment: Have a friend play the piano while you lie down on the floor next to it (preferably on a carpeted floor). You will feel the vibration of the music going through you. In the same way, the violet flame makes any object it touches sing its original keynote and returns it to its highest energy level of original perfection. The beautiful violet singing flame literally "sings" various melodies all day long as you send it here and there into all kinds of situations. It produces the sacred tone in all things, restoring everything to its original tone of life. Isn't that incredible?

Freedom to Love More

The violet flame is a joyous flame of freedom. Maybe you are beginning to see why. It restores everything and everyone to its highest form, down to every atom, cell, and electron. This is freedom, and it is the happiness and joy of a cosmos. The light of God flows more freely through you. Just think how much better you feel when you are filled with light! When you feel this light and freedom, you can contain more love and give more love. You are free to love everyone more. What a relief that will be!

Here is a mantra you can give so that the light of the violet flame can set you free.

Light, set me free!
Light, set me free! Light, set me free!
Light expand! Light expand!
Light expand, expand, expand!
Light I AM! Light I AM!
Light I AM, I AM, I AM!

I AM a being of violet fire,
I AM the purity God desires!

ACTIVITY #1:
Getting Unstuck

Goal: The goal of this activity is to show children how the violet flame can wash away all that makes them feel stuck, like those boulders of fear or pebbles of doubt in their world. This activity gives children a visual way to understand that they can use the violet flame when they are feeling out of sorts. The violet flame takes care of the molasses-like substance of our karma that slows us down. This activity will "stick" in children's minds, too.

Materials:
> Two small, clear glass or plastic containers
> A mix of clear and pink decorative stones
>   (available at craft stores)
> Violet decorative stones (available at craft stores)
> A small piece of purple cloth that can cover both small
>   containers
> Molasses
> A small pitcher

Preparation: Put the mix of clear and pink decorative stones in one container. Put the violet decorative stones in the other container. Place both containers under the purple cloth. Put molasses into the small pitcher so it can be poured easily. Also put the pitcher under the purple cloth.

The Activity: Bring the container with the mix of clear and pink decorative stones out from under the cloth and show the children. Try to have a sense of mystery and fun as you do this! Explain that these stones are like the red and white blood cells in our bodies. There are spaces in between the cells that can be filled with energy, which can be affected by our thoughts and feelings. Then bring out the pitcher of molasses. Slowly pour the molasses over the stones.

Explain that the black molasses represents negative feelings like fear and discouragement, etc. You can ask the children what kinds of feelings are hard for them. Give the container with the gooey "cells" to the children to look at closely and carefully pass around. The molasses coats the stones just like negative feelings can coat our physical cells, making us feel out of sorts. Ask the children if they think it is good to have our cells looking like that. What can help get rid of those feelings? The violet flame!

At this point the children can give the mantra, "I AM a being of violet fire! I AM the purity God desires!" (from chapter two) several times, or the "Light, Set Me Free!" mantra (given in this chapter).

Then bring out the other container with the violet stones in it. Do it with a sense of drama and fun, as if you are showing them something incredible! Then show the children the pretty violet stones and let them pass the container around to look at them. Explain that this is what cells look like after they have been bathed in the violet flame. They are sparkling. They are beautiful.

ACTIVITY #2:
Splat!

Goal: The goal of this activity is to teach children how to put the violet flame into anything that is bothering them and to show how the violet flame can dissolve problems. This is an outdoor, warm-weather activity.

Materials:

> Sidewalk chalk in many colors
> Many shades of violet-colored water balloons representing
>> various aspects of the violet flame (at least one for
>> each child)

Preparation: Fill the balloons with water.

The Activity: Have each child draw a simple picture of something he or she needs help resolving. Then give the children one or two water balloons each. When you are passing out the balloons, make it seem like you are giving them a special present that they should hold very carefully. They might giggle with the idea that a water balloon is a treasure!

Then tell the children that the water balloons represent the violet flame. Explain that the violet flame can dissolve all kinds of problems and burdens. If they want to, they can say something specific about their chalk picture that they would like the violet flame to help them with. Then they get to hurl the water balloons into their chalk drawing!

The dissolving of the image in chalk is the way negative thoughts and feelings can disappear with the violet flame. The water balloon might not dissolve the chalk drawing right away, just as problems might not immediately disappear with the violet flame. But if you keep throwing water balloons at the image, it dissolves. If you keep giving violet flame mantras, problems will dissolve bit by bit, according to the will of God.

ACTIVITY #3:
Violet-Flame Balloon Game

Goal: The goal of this activity is to enjoy the violet flame. If anyone is feeling stuck or out of sorts, this game will uplift them!

Materials:

Violet-colored balloons (one for each person)

Waltz music

Here is a link you might enjoy. It is Johann Strauss' "The Emperor Waltz."

https://www.youtube.com/watch?v=EBLaMmxyibE

Preparation: Gather the materials. Blow up all the balloons. Get the music ready and gather the people who will be doing this game. It is best to set this up in a room that doesn't have fragile items close by, or you can remove them before you begin. This game gets everyone moving!

The Activity: Start the waltz music and launch the balloons into the air. The goal is to keep all the balloons in the air for the entire song, but this is harder than it sounds. The joy of the waltz music and the balloons bouncing everywhere make this a great family activity.

CHAPTER FOUR

Fill Your Relationships with Joy!

"When I was a little girl, I discovered how extending my heart to my neighbors led to experiencing the joy of the violet flame."

Elizabeth Clare Prophet, *Violet Flame: Alchemy for Personal Change*

Relationships Are a Treasure

The relationships in your life can be one of your greatest blessings. Your time with your family and your friends can build wonderful memories. Good relationships can help us along life's road. How often has a kind word from a friend made you feel happy all day long? But just as the tides in the sea change from one moment to the next, relationships can also have their ups and downs.

Solving Sticky Problems

Our relationships can be our greatest opportunity to use the violet flame. When you ask for the violet flame to enrich your relationships or to solve a problem you have with someone, those relationships can be transformed. This is because the violet flame contains the qualities that help relationships the most—mercy, forgiveness, justice, tact, and diplomacy. And kindness is important too. Tact and diplomacy mean knowing what to say and do in a way that doesn't offend others and helps them to feel comfortable. You might know someone who tends to say things in a way that feels harsh or unkind. You would probably rather avoid that type of person. When you pray for the light of the violet flame to help with your relationships, there is a softening of the energy exchanged between you and others. This helps protect and deepen your relationships.

The Ups and Downs of Relationships

Most relationships have their ups and downs. For example, imagine that one minute you are having an exciting time with your best friend building a sand castle at the beach. It's the tallest and most beautiful sand castle you've ever built. You make tall turrets, winding moats, doorways, windows, and even a bridge and door made out of driftwood. Then your friend carelessly puts a pile of sand on the top of it to make another turret, but it's too heavy. Crash! Everything comes tumbling down. This is often the way a misunderstanding happens. Something small ruins things for a moment. You feel upset. Your friend feels upset. What can you do? The violet flame can help because it can bring harmony to these ups and downs that normally happen with friends and family. How does it do that?

The Gentleness of Mercy

Extending your heart to someone is often the best way to help a relationship. You might tell your friend that you know he didn't mean to topple your sand castle. You might say, "Let's use this *small* cup of sand next time so that we know it's just the right amount to put on the top." Then you can both go and create the most beautiful sand castle ever! Sometimes extending mercy might be hard to do. But both people benefit when a lovely river of mercy flows between them, sparkling with the light of their hearts. Your friendship can grow through mercy and forgiveness, which is the grace of the violet flame.

Extending mercy to someone can mean that you want to help your sister today, even though she did something mean to you yesterday. Maybe you realized that she was upset about something, which is why she took it out on you. You had compassion for her, so you didn't get upset. You might have even felt your heart bursting with love for your sister! Have you ever noticed how being merciful to someone can resolve a difficult situation more quickly? As mercy expands your heart, it frees everyone involved.

The Beauty of Forgiveness

The beauty of forgiveness is often intertwined with the gentle gift of mercy. When you forgive someone, you may lovingly forgive that person for doing the deed, but he or she still needs to make things right with you. For example, if your brother (or sister) accidentally drops your favorite book in the mud, what do you do? You might get mad at him, but you know it was an accident. He tells you he's sorry, and you forgive him freely.

But to make things right, your brother still needs to take care of the problem with the book, which is now ruined. He may either need to replace the book or give you the money to buy a new one. Sometimes we need to make things right by doing something to make up for what we did wrong. This is called justice, which is another quality of the violet flame. It is balancing what's wrong by making things right. But what if your brother is very little and can't afford to buy you a new book? Maybe he gives you all the money in his piggy bank, but it's only two dollars. Or maybe he buys you another book that he can afford. Sometimes that's ok too, because out of the forgiveness and mercy of your heart, you decide this is enough.

You can imagine that your little brother will feel very relieved when everything is ok between you again. You both might even end up laughing about it later. Forgiveness can be joyful, and the violet flame can help us forgive others more easily. When the violet flame floods us with compassion, it's easier to forgive others. How do you feel when you forgive someone? You usually feel better! You feel free because you aren't holding on to hurt feelings. Have you noticed that when you forgive others, they are free to forgive you too?

Karma in Relationships

Remember when we talked about karma a little bit earlier? Karma is the return to the sender of energy that he or she has sent forth. This return of energy means we receive back what we have sent out so that we can experience how that energy we sent out made others feel. For example, if we send out love, we get back love. If we send out anger, we get back the energy of anger in some way too. This helps us to learn from our mistakes and to balance our karma, while we also receive the blessings we are meant to receive.

When something happens between two people and karma is made, it creates a tie between them. A relationship that is positive for us may be very good karma. This is the best friend who brings sunshine to our day. At other times we may have negative karma with someone. This is the person we have a hard time getting along with, and this karma needs to be resolved at some point. Have you ever felt that someone rubs you the wrong way? If so, there could be a little bit of karma that needs to be worked out with that person.

There is a saying that goes "The only person you can change is yourself." Well, if you call for the violet flame, the first person who is transformed is you! When the dazzling violet flame enters your heart, it works to transmute the karma you have with others. It also opens your heart to receive the many qualities of the violet flame right within you—and then your relationships improve! How does this happen?

When you ask for the violet flame to solve these sticky situations with people, you may find that your reaction to this person softens or you have a breakthrough in understanding. The violet flame can saturate the situation with love, forgiveness, and mercy. The justice of the violet flame also plays a part, because sometimes situations need to be made right between people, as in the story above. Saying "I'm sorry" can help a lot too. Even if you have a hard time forgiving someone and you don't want to continue a relationship with him or her, you can still love the soul and hope the best for that person. When this happens, there is lightness and joy instead of a sense of burden and struggle.

Violet-Flame Spheres

Here is a fun thing you can do to help resolve problems in relationships. You can send violet-flame spheres of mercy and forgiveness to anyone you would like to send them to. You can send these spheres by saying a simple prayer, such as "Dear God, please send violet-flame spheres to [_____]." You can send these spheres to anyone, past, present, or future. You can send them to people you knew when you were younger or to someone you don't like so much now. You can send them to your neighbors, your teachers, and even the teacher you're going to have next year. You can send them to anyone you know where your relationship with them could use some improvement. Here is a picture of violet-flame spheres to help you see them in your mind as you send out these beautiful spheres.

The Violet Flame Is a Cosmic Eraser

When you go to school, you carry an eraser in your backpack for erasing mistakes. When we need help with our life lessons that come to us each day, we need a "cosmic eraser" to erase our karma as well as the problems that come up—including in our relationships. The violet flame *is* a cosmic eraser!

One way this "eraser" works is to send mercy and forgiveness to anyone you may have hurt or who has hurt you. The power of mercy and forgiveness is amazing! Justice is also amazing, because God will take care of these problems through the justice of his law. That means that we don't have to worry about getting back at anyone for something they did to us. God will take care of it through the law of karma.

Now, can you imagine a big violet-flame eraser rubbing away problems in your relationships? Maybe you can imagine this right now, as you say the following mantra on forgiveness.

I AM forgiveness acting here,
Casting out all doubt and fear,
Setting men forever free
With wings of cosmic victory.

I AM calling in full power
For forgiveness every hour;
To all life in every place
I flood forth forgiving grace.

FUN FAMILY ACTIVITIES

ACTIVITY #1:
Create Violet-Flame Bouquets

Goal: The goal of this activity is to make bouquets from real or silk flowers for the dinner table or as a gift for a friend or loved one. While you and your child are making the bouquets, you both secretly know that the qualities of mercy and forgiveness of the violet flame will help your family and friends.

Materials:

      Fresh or silk flowers in shades of violet, purple, pink, and lavender
      Fresh or silk greenery to fill out the arrangement (optional)
      Vase or container
      Scissors to trim flowers to the right length
      String or yarn to tie around the bouquet if it is a gift

Preparation: Gather the materials and set them up on a table.

The Activity: Explain to your child that you're going to create a special violet-flame bouquet. Allow the child to select the flowers and then arrange them in the vase or tie them with a piece of string. While the child is giving the bouquets to others, the child can imagine how the violet flame will help create new friendships and renew old ones. Children can also feel good that their gifts of the violet flame are helping others and lightening their day.

ACTIVITY #2:
Violet-Flame Spheres

Goal: The goal of this activity is to make violet-flame "spheres" so children can visualize them while doing the Forgiveness mantra. They can toss them too!

Materials:

> 6" violet paper plates (available at party stores)
>
> White paper for wings
>
> Scissors
>
> Glue
>
> Cotton balls (optional)
>
> Pen

Preparation: Gather the materials and set them up on a table. You might want to spread newspapers on the table for this project. Draw and cut out many white wings ahead of time, using the picture in this chapter as a guide.

The Activity: Glue a wing on each side of the plate. If you want to make the wings fluffy, you can glue cotton onto the wings. You can write the names of family or friends on the plates. Then explain that while the plates are flat, violet-flame spheres are round like balls.

Everyone can toss the plates as they give the Forgiveness mantra. Even though this is a fun activity, children can also see this as a spiritual exercise of sending love and mercy to those they think need it most.

ACTIVITY #3:
An "Uplifting" Violet-Flame Gift

Goal: The goal of this activity is to give love and encouragement to others in a fun way and to experience the joy of giving.

Materials:

Helium balloons in shades of violet, one for each person
(Regular balloons also work, but helium ones are more exciting.)
Violet ribbon
Violet-colored pens or markers
Small pieces of paper
Tape

Preparation: Collect the supplies and decide on who will be the recipients of these "uplifting" gifts. It could be someone who needs some special love or encouragement. Talk to your child about someone they know who might need a little boost or extra care. The gift could also be for someone your child has had a challenge with in some way.

The Activity: Have your child write a note of kindness and encouragement on a piece of paper. Attach a violet ribbon to a balloon and then tape the note to the ribbon. Deliver the balloons and watch the violet flame of joy fill the air!

SPECIAL FAMILY RITUALS

Another quality of the violet flame is ritual. If you think about your day, from the minute you wake up until the time you go to bed, you know that there is one thing you can count on: the sun will rise and the sun will set, as it always does and always will. This is ritual. It is the ritual of the cosmos, which brings order to our lives and helps us know what to plan for and what to expect each day. The reason ritual is another quality of the violet flame and of the seventh ray is because any cycle we begin is fulfilled by ritual in the seventh and last ray. We can also think of the word *ritual* as *right-you-all*—meaning "righting of the energies."

We all have rituals in our lives, such as eating our meals at a certain time each day and watching our favorite TV show in the evening. You may have a specific time and place to do your homework, you may look forward to a regular snack before bedtime, and you hopefully always say your prayers before going to bed. These are rituals that bring order and comfort to us. Birthday parties, fireworks on the Fourth of July, and trick-or-treating at Halloween are also rituals that bring comfort and a sense of order to our lives.

Rituals also bring people together, which nurture and strengthen our relationships. When we do things with our family, we feel that we belong together and that we can share our thoughts and feelings. This helps us feel happy and fulfilled.

The following is an activity you can do with your family that is fun as well as helpful for everyone's spiritual path.

Put Your Worries into the Flame!

[To parents:] Gather your family members around a campfire or your fireplace. As everyone sits by the fire, let them feel and appreciate the fire's gentle heat and comforting presence. While all are enjoying the warmth of the fire, have everyone imagine that this flame is a beautiful violet flame.

Using the violet flame as a focus for discussion, invite all family members to talk about the blessings or challenges that each one is experiencing. This could take minutes or hours, depending on how deep the discussion goes. Once everyone has had a chance to talk, ask each family member to "throw" all of their cares and concerns into the flame. This can include anything that anyone would like to get rid of. It could be feelings of their own, like worries, fears, frustrations, etc., or it could be something that someone else has said or done that was upsetting and needs resolution.

Anything that is unwanted can go into the flame. Some people may want to "throw" so many things into the flame that they look like a baseball pitcher! When we put a concern into the violet flame, we trust that God will take care of the situation according to his will. We can then go to bed in peace, feeling that we are right with ourselves and right with God.

Such Polite Children You Have!

Grace and courtesy are also qualities of the violet flame, which are aspects of tact and diplomacy. A person who expresses graciousness is often most courteous, compassionate, understanding, and mindful not to offend others. We might also call this having good manners. Here are a few exercises for children to practice their manners, bringing them and all around them closer to what we might imagine as the very culture of heaven!

The Family Meal

Regular family meals are an important ritual for the purpose of strengthening family relationships. It is also a time for boys and girls of all ages to learn the many details of daily etiquette. The following are some ideas:

- Children can help set the table, learning where the silverware goes, where the glasses are placed, etc. This can be especially fun when company is coming and for special occasions.
- There are many details that can be taught and practiced, such as placing the napkin on one's lap, saying "please" and "thank you" when passing the food, and having proper voice levels.

It's important to explain that etiquette is for the purpose of helping everyone at the table feel comfortable and thus able to enjoy their meal. Teaching children etiquette is a fun way to share in the comforts and joys of a special meal with others. There are many resources for this online. Here are a few to get you started:

https://www.verywell.com/teaching-kids-good-table-manners-620306
https://www.youtube.com/watch?v=mgZeziVUsZ0
https://www.pinterest.co.uk/mycowtownlife/etiquette-class-for-kids

Children Love Tea Parties

As a variation to the family meal, children can be in charge of their own table gathering by having a tea party! They can even be chefs and waitresses or waiters. They can invite all of their family members and more, and they can dress up in their finest. Children can learn dress etiquette, table manners, how to properly drink tea or other beverages, and how to carry on a polite conversation. They can also learn how it feels to be graciously responsible for their guests, helping them feel comfortable with one another. (Using the above website resources will be helpful.)

Out on the Town

After children have practiced their dinner etiquette, you might take the whole family out to a fancy restaurant as a reward for everyone's hard work. ("Fancy" can be any restaurant that is not your ordinary place to eat.) This will give the children a chance to dress up, to order their meal on their own, and to practice all of the aspects of manners and graciousness that they've learned. You may want to arrange this event with management so they can be a part of your experience.

CHAPTER FIVE

The Secret Ingredient for Change

*"We can all use the violet flame. We can all use change.
We can all use transmutation. If we can't use it, then we're
really stultified. We're stuck in the mud. We're down in the mud
and the mire and we can't move. But if we can use it, then, you
see, God has the power to free us. And when he frees us, we go
up—we are no longer confined to the sense of limitation."*

Elizabeth Clare Prophet, *The Lost Teachings of Jesus*

The Alchemy of Change

Most people would like to change something in their life. Maybe you do too! You might want to get a dog, live closer to a park, or fly in an airplane for the first time. You might like to have more patience and be nicer to your brother or sister. You might also like to feel closer to God in your heart. Another word for change is *alchemy*, which means the process of changing something ordinary into something special. (More on this in chapter six.)

Sometimes change is dramatic, like in the movie *Beauty and the Beast* when the Beast finally becomes human again. Now, that is an unforgettable change! You might not want to experience change while being suspended in the air and surrounded by blinding light, like the Beast did. But is there anything you want to change in your life that isn't quite as dramatic as this? Usually change takes work. What if you could experience change in your life more easily? What if you had a secret ingredient to help you? Again, that secret ingredient is the violet flame!

Restoring What's Meant to Be

The violet flame clears away the obstacles so that what is meant to happen in your life can come about. You might be wondering what this means and how this happens. Well, it means that God has a plan for you, your life, and all that's meant to be for your greatest joy and the victory of your soul. We can call this your divine plan. Isn't that comforting? You may have heard people say, "I was meant to be a doctor" or

"My husband and I were meant to be together." When people say this about something that's happened in their lives, it shows that they are aware that certain things happen because it's part of God's plan.

God knows you so well that he knows what's best for you. He has a plan for you to fulfill so that your soul stays right on track. You might think of this plan as a map or a blueprint. A blueprint, as you may know, is a plan showing what something should be when it's completed. You may have seen blueprints for a building that's being built. It shows people exactly how it needs to be made so it's sturdy and safe. When you're in tune with this special plan that God has for you, you feel wonderful. You feel like skipping—maybe even jumping—because everything in your life feels right. And do you know what? The closer you feel to God, the greater your connection is with him and the easier it is to know what's in that plan!

When you pray for the violet flame, it automatically changes, or transmutes, all that is not in harmony with your special plan. So if you're meant to be a concert pianist, for example, you can be sure that God will help you find the time to practice! The violet flame will clear away the obstacles, just like the rocks on the path that we talked about in chapter three. When this is done, the best possible outcome in any situation is likely to come about. When those blocks are removed, new opportunities abound.

Change Can Be Good!

Have you ever had a good friend move to another town or have your favorite teacher move to another class? Sometimes we don't like change. We often like things to stay just the way they are. However, change is a constant in life, whether we like it or not! The more we work toward positive change in our lives, the better we usually feel.

When we pray for the violet flame, we are bringing into our life the light of the will of God. This helps assure us that even though change can be challenging, changes that we don't like at the time can actually turn out well in the end. Again, the story of *Beauty and the Beast* is a good example. When Belle fell in love with the Beast even though he was horribly ugly, it proved to the Beast how much she loved him for who he was inside. Because of this, he was able to return to being a prince. So in the end, maybe everything turned out for the better.

The Love of God and the Will of God

Do you like to paint and mix colors together to see what colors you can make? When you mix blue and pink together, you know that it makes the color violet. What do you think will happen if you put in a little more pink or a little more blue? Most likely what will happen is that you'll get a shade of violet that's on the pinker side, or you'll get a shade of violet that's on the bluer side, closer to purple.

Well, here's something else that's interesting about the violet flame. When we think of these colors in terms of the light and energy of God, we can understand that when the violet flame is on the pinker side, it contains a greater portion of God's love and mercy. When the violet flame is on the bluer side, it contains a greater portion of God's will, strength, and protection, which brings us closer to our divine plan. This explains the value of those many shades of violet we talked about earlier.

With all of this love of God and the will of God contained within the many shades of violet, no wonder the violet flame can do so much to bring about positive change in our lives!

Visualization Is a Key for Change

Another important thing to know about change is that it's helpful to visualize what it is that you're hoping and praying for. Do you know what visualization means? If you close your eyes and concentrate on seeing a picture in your mind about something, that is visualization. If you can see something in your mind's eye that you would like to have happen, it can come about more quickly (if it's meant to be, of course). Let's try it. Maybe you would like to have a new bike. Close your eyes and imagine just what that bike would look like. What color is it? What style is it? How does it feel when you touch it? See yourself riding it down your street, going here and there on your new bike. Maybe you wave at your friends as you ride by. The more clearly you can visualize what you want to have happen, and the more fully you can feel it has already happened, the better.

If you add your secret ingredient of the violet flame to this formula for change, you can bring desired change to all areas of your life more quickly and easily. You can visualize the violet flame in, through, and around anything you want to see changed, dissolving negativity and changing the entire situation. Sometimes change takes time, so it's helpful to also be patient while waiting to see what happens.

Violet, Purple, Pink...

The following is a simple mantra you can give so that you feel filled with light, closer to God, and closer to fulfilling your special plan. This mantra is really fun to visualize, because you can imagine all of the shades of violet that you can come up with when mixing your paints together. Since this mantra includes this variety of color, it will bring more of the light of God's will into your world, helping you to bring desired change into your life.

Violet, purple, pink,
Flash through that I may think:
God's in me—I AM free
Now and for eternity!

Violet, purple, pink,
Help me now to drink
Electric hue, flashing through
Into all I think and say and do!

To bring change into your life, you can take certain steps. You can take the practical steps you need to do to make something happen. Then you add the violet flame, along with visualization, to make those changes happen more quickly, easily, and according to God's plan. Have fun!

FUN FAMILY ACTIVITIES

ACTIVITY #1:
Squish! Violet-Flame Goo

Goal: The goal of this activity is to show that the violet flame is made up of the blue flame and the pink flame together. Transmutation and change through the violet flame happens through dedication to God's will (blue flame) and through the light of God's love (pink flame), which work together to bring about the wondrous alchemies of God's heart.

Materials:
> Cornstarch and water
> Cooking pot and stove
> Blue and red food coloring
> Two bowls
> Sandwich-size plastic bags that zip closed

Preparation: Make a batch of cornstarch in the cooking pot according to directions. The amount you make will depend on how many children will be doing the activity. Two tablespoons of prepared cornstarch "goo" should be enough for each child. After making the batch of plain cornstarch, separate it into two portions and place each portion in a bowl. Add blue food coloring to one bowl of goo and mix until thoroughly blended. Add red food coloring to the other bowl of goo and mix until thoroughly blended. The result should be a pink-colored goo. Then place one tablespoon of each into the plastic bags. No matter how tempting it may be, do not mix the two together—this is for the children to do!

The Activity: Distribute the plastic bags to the children, each with the two blobs of goo in them. Explain that the violet flame is a mixture of the blue flame of God's will and the pink flame of God's love. Ask each child to squish the goo together in the bags to create violet-flame goo! This is a wonderful hands-on activity that is a lot of fun for children of all ages.

ACTIVITY #2:
Treasure Mapping for Change

Goal: The goal of this activity is to make a treasure map to help bring about desired change for all members of the family. A treasure map is a great addition to the spiritual work of the violet flame. This can be a good time for families to work on a goal together, such as buying a new car or going on a special vacation.

Materials:

> Poster board
> Magazines and pictures
> Spiritual pictures of your choice
> Glue sticks
> Scissors
> Magic markers, pens, and pencils

Preparation: Collect the materials. Have one piece of poster board for each participant, or one board for the entire family. The poster board can be white, but you can also use other colors for whatever you are trying to manifest. For example, for greater abundance, green would be an excellent choice. For greater love, a pink poster board would work well, etc. This activity is done most easily at a large table so everyone can share the magazines and pictures.

The Activity: A treasure map represents our highest goals and aspirations. It helps us manifest our goals because we can see and visualize them clearly. Each person can cut out photographs or pictures of things they would like in their lives. Colored pictures work best because the subconscious responds faster to color. These could be physical objects or representations of spiritual goals.

In the center of the poster board, place a representation of what you consider to be the source of your goals and abundance. This could be a spiritual picture, such as the Chart of Your Divine Self (see chapter seven). Then each person can find the pictures of objects, circumstances, or spiritual qualities that he or she wants to manifest. Each person can glue their pictures on their own poster board or on the family board. When the treasure maps are done, they can be used as a focus during family prayer time or hung in a place often seen by the treasure-mappers. It's important to look at your treasure map every day, even several times a day.

One wonderful story about treasure mapping is how Mark Prophet made a scrapbook and cut out a picture he had found in a magazine of a boy like himself and put it on one page. On the other page he pasted a picture of a girl about six years old. This was his dream girl! Later, Elizabeth Clare Prophet saw the picture of the girl and realized that it looked very much like she did when she was six years old!

ACTIVITY #3:
Violet-Flame Meditations

Goal: Visualizations are a magnet that attract creative energies to us. The goal of this activity is to help children learn how to focus their minds on what they are hoping for.

Materials:
>A quiet space
>Calm music appropriate for meditation

Preparation: Create a quiet place, with no distractions. Play some relaxing music that will help the child relax and go within his or her heart.

The Activity: Meditation can happen in several ways. One way is to sit quietly and meditate on deep breathing for several minutes with eyes closed. Another way is to look at violet-flame pictures or objects. The child can also visualize themselves surrounded by a gently blazing violet flame, comforting the child while being bathed in the love and will of God. (The length of time a child can sit and meditate depends, of course, on the age and attention span of the child.)

CHAPTER SIX

Saint Germain, Our Friend and Brother

"I have experienced the tremendous love of Saint Germain in so many personal ways. His gift of the violet flame is truly the greatest way we can all become free and make the world a better place."

Elizabeth Clare Prophet, *Violet Flame: Alchemy for Personal Change*

Friends Help Us along the Way

A faithful friend is a joy in life. A true friend can be your parent, your brother or sister, someone in your class, or just about anyone—but a true friend is always someone you can trust. A true friend keeps your deepest secrets. It's the person you can confide in and who loves you no matter what you do. Like Pooh and Piglet in *Winnie the Pooh,* we all need friends who always want the best for us. Do you have a friend like this?

The Ascended Masters Are Our Friends

Here is a wonderful thought: There are many friends in heaven who love us as much as our closest friends on earth do. These friends are called ascended masters. We can also think of them as the saints in heaven. Jesus is an ascended master. Many people talk to Jesus every day. They thank him when they feel grateful. They talk to him when they feel sad. Mother Mary is another ascended master, and many people devotedly pray the rosary to her every day. There are so many ascended masters who want to help us. If you look up into the deep night sky and see millions of bright stars, you have an idea of how many beings of light there are.

You might wonder how someone all the way up in heaven could possibly understand your problems. But these masters have lived on earth too. They also had challenges and had to balance their karma so that they could stay in heaven permanently. Even though they had difficulties while they were on earth, just like us, they had so much light in their hearts that they were able to conquer situations with love. They earned the right to ascend to heaven, just like Jesus and the many saints in heaven have done. To ascend means that we go to heaven and no longer need to have our physical body. When we ascend, we have a beautiful body of pure light, just like the ascended masters. Did you know that you are meant to ascend too? That is part of God's plan for all of us.

The ascension from our earthly body to our heavenly body usually happens after many lifetimes, when we have finished everything we need to do here on earth. Earth is like a school-room. We learn our lessons here, and when we finish them and pass our tests, we can become an ascended master. Having many lifetimes and coming back to earth again and again is called reembodiment, or reincarnation.

You Will Love the Ascended Master Saint Germain!

The ascended masters, who are in heaven now, would like to help us become ascended masters in any way they can. There is one loving master who is very special because he is the first one to teach us about the violet flame. And he is an expert on teaching us how to use it! It is his specialty! Think about something you do very well. The violet flame is like that for this master. His name is Saint Germain, and he loves you. He knows that the violet flame can bring miracles to you if you ask.

Saint Germain's name means "holy brother." He is a loving, gracious, merciful, and forgiving ascended master. He embodies the freedom flame. You will never find a better friend than Saint Germain! Like other masters, he has had many lifetimes on earth. Saint Germain has been a guiding light—a mystic, alchemist, scientist, philosopher, monk, prophet, and more. You have probably heard of him before as someone he was in other lifetimes. Some of his lifetimes were Christopher Columbus, Merlin, Francis Bacon, and others. He has been working from heaven for many centuries to help establish freedom on earth. Even after his ascension in the year 1684, he appeared throughout the eighteenth- and nineteenth-century courts as the Wonderman of Europe in order to help establish freedom there. This didn't work very well, but at least one good thing came out of it.

Saint Germain Inspired the Creation of the Waltz

When Saint Germain realized that his efforts to establish freedom in Europe weren't working, he took up another plan. He inspired musician Johann Strauss to write the Strauss waltzes. Do you remember when we talked about the waltz earlier? Well, here's something very interesting about that. Waltz music carries the rhythm of the violet flame, which is in three-quarter time! You may have heard some of this beautiful waltz music before. It's so lovely that it makes you want to whirl across the room! Saint Germain's plan was that when people danced to the music of the waltz, they would actually be bringing forth the violet flame without even realizing it. This helped anchor the flame of freedom in Europe, even though his original efforts had failed. What a good plan!

You Can Visit Saint Germain in His Retreat

One way to become closer to Saint Germain and other ascended masters is to visit them at night in their retreats. A retreat is like a home for the ascended masters in heaven and a place where they work with other masters and the many students who visit them. Saint Germain, like many ascended masters, has a retreat in the spiritual plane beyond this physical world. We can't see these places with our physical eyes. But when we sleep at night, we can travel in our finer bodies to visit them. Some people remember these beautiful places of light. These retreats have classrooms, meeting rooms, and council halls. You can visit meditation rooms, laboratories, and even amphitheaters where the masters can show you how the violet flame works to clear up records of past lifetimes.

Saint Germain's own special retreat is called the Cave of Symbols. It's in Table Mountain in the Rocky Mountains. It has a vaulted chamber that is two hundred feet wide and covered with stalactites of rainbow hues in the formation of mystic symbols. He also teaches classes at the Royal Teton Retreat, which is congruent with the Teton Range near Jackson Hole, Wyoming. You can ask Saint Germain to take you to these retreats and to teach you more about the gift of the sparkling, life-changing violet flame. You can say a prayer before you go to bed, asking to be taken to a certain retreat. In this prayer you can fill in the blank with anything you need help with:

"Beloved Saint Germain, please take me to your retreat tonight and teach me about the violet flame. Please help me learn how to use it in the following situation: [_____]. I thank you and accept it done according to God's will. Amen."

Saint Germain's Greatest Gift

Our friend and teacher, Saint Germain, has given much to the world during his many lifetimes, but the knowledge of the violet flame is his greatest gift of the ages. He wants to help us balance our karma quickly and easily so we can be closer to God in our hearts. He knew centuries ago that it would take us a very long time to balance the karma from our many embodiments if we didn't have the violet flame to help us. That's why it's so important to him that we have it and use it.

Saint Germain also gave us a valentine! It is the following mantra, which is a way to be close to Saint Germain and to call for his violet flame. Isn't it cool to think that an ascended master sent us a valentine? Saint Germain is a wonderful friend who will be with you through anything. Take this gift from his heart and keep him close to you as you discover more about the violet flame.

I AM the light of the heart,
Shining in the darkness of being
And changing all into the golden treasury
Of the mind of Christ.

I AM projecting my love
Out into the world
To erase all errors
And to break down all barriers.

I AM the power of infinite love,
Amplifying itself
Until it is victorious,
World without end!

FUN FAMILY ACTIVITIES

ACTIVITY #1:
Souvenirs of the Cave of Symbols

Goal: The goal of this activity is to create stalactites and stalagmites. (Read the brief description of the Cave of Symbols retreat from this chapter, noting that there are rainbow-colored stalactites in the retreat.) This link will provide a detailed description of the activity, with photographs and helpful tips:

http://www.sciencekidsathome.com/science_experiments/growing_stalactites.html

AUTHOR DANIEL FRANCISCO MADRIGAL MÖLLER

ACTIVITY #2:
Have a Waltz!

Goal: The goal of this activity is to introduce family and friends to the beauty of the waltz.

Materials:

Decorations

Waltz music

Preparations:

Decide on a good-sized room to hold your waltz.

Invite your family and friends.

Have your child(ren) decide on how they would like to decorate this space, and have them help.

Establish a few designated people to teach others how to waltz.

Play Strauss waltzes. You might enjoy the following link. This is Johann Strauss' "The Blue Danube."

https://www.youtube.com/watch?v=lDaJ7rFg66A

Activity: Have Fun!

ACTIVITY #3:
Create a Skit from a Shakespeare Play

Goal: The goal of this activity is for children to become familiar with the Shakespeare plays, which Saint Germain wrote in his embodiment as Francis Bacon. Francis Bacon was a brilliant writer and dramatist. Children can create short skits and act out portions of these plays. Older children could even act out an abbreviated version of an entire play.

Materials:

    Books on Shakespeare plays

    (An excellent book for children is *Tales from Shakespeare,*
        by Charles and Mary Lamb.)

    Paper and pen for children to plan the script

    A "stage" and props to act out the play

    Several children (or adults) to participate

Activity: Enjoy watching the play with family and friends!

**Please see the following link for a beautiful coloring sheet
on Saint Germain.**

https://www.summitlighthouse.org/SaintGermainPage

CHAPTER SEVEN

The Light of God Is within You

*"If you can imagine the center of your mighty
I AM Presence as an infinite galaxy of light, you begin
to think about a new perception of the Infinite One....
This would be the individual, as you, clearly manifest
as a ray of light coalesced in this dimension."*

Elizabeth Clare Prophet, *Pearls of Wisdom*, vol. 24, no. 47

The Miracle of Alchemy

In the last chapter you met our friend and brother, Saint Germain. He is the wonderful master of the violet flame. Saint Germain is also the master of the sacred science of alchemy, which we talked about in chapter five. You may have heard of this word *alchemy* even before reading this book. When some people hear this word, they may think of Merlin from the days of King Arthur, who wore a tall pointed hat and heated potions over a flame. What does this word mean to you?

Medieval alchemists attempted to change base metals into gold by using heat. However, their idea of transmuting, or changing, matter had a deeper spiritual meaning that is often forgotten today. This alchemical process symbolizes changing our human self into our Divine Self. You can become an alchemist right at home, right now, by using the violet flame. And you won't even need a special hat!

The Greatest Alchemy of All

Alchemy is wonderful because it can bring you to the golden moment of your ultimate reunion with God. This change is the greatest alchemy of all. Do you remember how you feel after you've been away on a trip and return to your house? You might have had a great adventure at Disney World or camping. After all this excitement it feels good to be home again, doesn't it? Reunion with God will feel like going home again in a bigger way. You will feel light and free!

This alchemy of reunion with God is a process that happens day by day, moment by moment. For example, when you choose to remain silent when you're tempted to say something bad about someone, this is the alchemy of changing the lesser self into the greater Self. When you take time to talk with someone who needs a little cheering up even though you'd rather be with your friends, this is also changing that lesser self into the greater Self. This is the alchemy of becoming one with God in your heart.

We want to return to God because we came from God. But God is not an old man sitting up in the clouds! What many people don't realize is that the spirit and energy of God is already everywhere in nature's power and beauty, and it is inside of them as well.

Again, think about how you feel as you look up into the night sky. You see millions of stars sparkling in a river of light. It is our own Milky Way galaxy. Does it give you a sense of wonder when you look at it? The energy of God makes galaxies spin in the velvety night sky—and he created all of it! How is it possible that this same energy is in you? This idea can seem almost impossible, but it's true.

One way to think about this is to consider a tiny drop of water from the ocean. If you taste it, it is salty. All the elements that are in that wide blue ocean are also in a single drop of water. In the same way, the Spirit of God is in you. You are as a drop in the ocean of God! Isn't that wonderful to think about?

If this union with God is so important, how can we have it? How can the violet flame help us? As we have learned in earlier chapters, the violet flame has the power to change us. As you also know, the violet flame helps us balance our karma. It purifies our hearts and allows us to become freer and freer of that lesser self. The violet flame helps us reunite with God by helping resolve the karmic patterns of how we've used our energy in the past. It helps us rise higher in thought and feeling each day as we think about becoming closer to God. It will help us get there more quickly, more easily, and with a lot more joy.

The Chart of Your Divine Self

You might like a way to picture God in your mind as you think about all of this. You know what you look like physically because you can see yourself in the mirror each day. But it's harder to know what you look like spiritually. That's why the ascended masters have given us a beautiful diagram of our inner spiritual Self. This picture is called the Chart of Your Divine Self. The upper figure in the Chart is called the I AM Presence, your individualized Presence of God that is right within you.

The brilliantly colored rings around the center of the upper figure are called the causal body, which you will learn about soon. The center figure in the Chart is called your Holy Christ

Self, also called your Higher Self. Jesus showed us the example of being the Christ so that we can become the Christ too. The Christ Self is the mediator between your I AM Presence and you. Have you ever had an experience when a little voice inside you told you what to do, or what *not* to do? That little voice inside is your Holy Christ Self trying to help you do the right thing.

You might be wondering where you are in this Chart. There you are, as the lower figure in the Chart, surrounded by the dazzling violet flame. The stream of light that you see coming from your I AM Presence to your Holy Christ Self and then to you is called the crystal cord. This is how the light comes down from your I AM Presence to your heart. The ascended masters want us to remember how important the violet flame is for us. That's why the lower figure in the Chart is surrounded by violet flame.

You Have Your Very Own Star

Those colorful rings around the center of the upper figure in the Chart make up what's called your causal body. The causal body is like having your very own bank account in heaven! You can think of your lovely causal body as your very own star. All those stars you see at night remind us of the causal bodies of great beings of light. Your own star—your causal body—shines brightly too! Every good deed you've ever done in any lifetime goes up to your causal body. Just think! God never forgets the good things that you do or have done in this or past lives. These honorable deeds as well as the talents you develop increase the size of the distinct color bands that you see in the upper figure of the Chart.

For example, if you express your love in some way to a person in need, that energy goes up to the pink band of your causal body and makes it larger. If you are a doctor or a nurse and help people get well, that energy goes up to the green band of your causal body, which will increase. If you study hard and learn new things, the yellow band of your causal body will also increase. This happens with all the good things you do in your life. So when your heart is open and the light is flowing freely within you because you are calling for the violet flame, you will probably do many wonderful things and increase the size of your causal body!

And here is another very interesting thing to know: Your causal body will be different from your best friend's causal body because you are very different people. You might love science, while your friend might love art. Do you have something that you can do exceptionally well, almost effortlessly? This could be a sign that you've done this particular thing quite well in other lifetimes, which is why you have that ability now. It comes easily for you.

Mark Prophet had some helpful observations about the causal body. He was a very practical man and loved to make spiritual concepts easy to understand. He reminded us that the causal body pictured in the Chart is not actually flat. It is a sphere. Mark compared the causal body to a huge grapefruit! He said that your causal body is a shining sphere of pulsating light, with your I AM Presence in the center of it. This is how Mark Prophet, with his great sense of humor, made the Chart of Your Divine Self more real for everyone. It was his way of helping people feel closer to their I AM Presence.

The Tube of Light to Protect You

There is something simple you can do each day to be closer to your I AM Presence right now. Do you see that white cylinder of light in the Chart that goes from the I AM Presence and down around the person surrounded by violet flame? This is called your tube of light. You can say a short mantra, or decree, to have this tube of light around you each day. It will protect and seal you. The violet flame inside it will help you stay close to your I AM Presence and Holy Christ Self.

You can start becoming an alchemist by giving the following decree, which will seal you in your own tube of light. It will enfold you with the dazzling violet flame. Remember that every time you say the words "I AM," you are talking about your I AM Presence. You are saying "God in me is." As you say these words, imagine a cylinder of light coming down around you. It is nine feet in diameter and it goes three feet below your feet. And remember, too, that it's important to visualize what you are praying for so that your prayer is more effective.

Beloved I AM Presence bright,
Round me seal your tube of light
From ascended master flame
Called forth now in God's own name.
Let it keep my temple free
From all discord sent to me.

I AM calling forth violet fire
To blaze and transmute all desire,
Keeping on in freedom's name
Till I AM one with the violet flame.

Your magnificent tube of light, filled with the violet flame, is a simple tool that will seal and protect you all day long. As you pursue the violet flame, you are using the power of the spoken Word to achieve the greatest alchemy of all, which is your reunion with God.

SPECIAL STORY AND ACTIVITY

[To parents:] The following is a story to read to your child that beautifully describes the concept of being a drop in the ocean of God, which is covered in this chapter. As you read this together, it may be helpful to encourage a sense of reverence and awe as the story unfolds. After you have finished reading, you can duplicate the experience described in the story (simple directions follow). This tale is summarized from Chandogya Upanishad:

A Drop in the Ocean of God

"Believe me, my son," said Svetaketu's father, a sage. *"An invisible and subtle essence is the Spirit of the whole Universe. That is Reality. That is Atman. Thou Art That."*

"Explain more to me, father," said Svetaketu.

"So be it, my son. Place this lump of salt in water and return tomorrow morning."

Svetaketu did as he was commanded.

In the morning his father asked him to take out the lump of salt. Svetaketu looked into the water, but could not find the salt, as it had dissolved.

His father then said, "Taste the water. How is it?"

"It is salty," replied Svetaketu.

"Look for the salt again," the father directed.

"I cannot see the salt, father. I only see water that tastes salty," commented Svetaketu.

Svetaketu's father then said, "In the same way, O my son, you cannot see the Spirit. But in truth he is here. An invisible and subtle essence is the Spirit of the whole Universe. That is Reality. That is Truth. Thou Art That (Twam Tat Asi)."

ACTIVITY:
Your Very Own "Ocean"

Goal: To demonstrate for the child the concept explained in this chapter, that God is like the ocean and we are each like a drop of water containing all of the same elements that make up the ocean.

Materials:
> A clear glass of water
> Salt
> A dropper or spoon

Preparation: Place items on a table.

The Activity: Mix the salt into the water, wait for a period of time, then have your child taste the water. Explain the teaching that is described in the story.

FUN FAMILY ACTIVITIES

ACTIVITY #1:
Violet, Purple, Pink Snow Globe

Goal: The goal of this activity is to create a snow globe with a figure that is surrounded by the sparkling violet flame, just as you see the lower figure surrounded by this same spiritual fire in the Chart of Your Divine Self.

Materials:

> A small jar with a tight-fitting lid (baby food jars work well)
> Violet, purple, and pink glitter
> A small plastic or ceramic figure of a person
>> (metal will rust so do not use)
> Hot glue gun
> Sandpaper
> Oil-based enamel paint
> Distilled water
> Glycerin (can be purchased at drug stores)

Preparation: Gather the materials and set them up on a table or other work space.

The Activity: First, unscrew the lid from the jar and paint it with the oil-based enamel paint in the color of your choice. After the paint is dry, turn the lid over so the inside of it is facing upward. Sand the inside of the lid with the sandpaper. Then attach your plastic figure to the inside of the lid using the hot glue gun, gluing the feet to the inside of the lid. While the glue is drying, fill the jar almost to the top with distilled water. Add a pinch of glycerin and some violet-flame glitter. The glycerin will prevent the glitter from falling too fast. Be sure not to add too much glitter because it will just stick to the bottom of the jar when it is turned over.

When the glue is dry, screw the lid on the jar tightly. Be careful not to bump your figure. Then turn the jar over, shake gently, and watch the violet flame swirl, sparkle, and dance. (If needed, the details for this project can be found on www.marthastewart.com.)

ACTIVITY #2:
Violet-Flame Galaxy Mobile

Goal: The goal of this activity is to create a beautiful violet-flame mobile to remind us of the energy of God in the galaxies of cosmos.

Materials:
> Blank CD discs (without a label), one for each child
> Artificial gems or sequins in various shades of violet
> Glue
> String

Preparation: Collect the materials and set them up on a table or other work space.

The Activity: Explain that you are going to each create a galaxy of violet flame for the children to hang in their rooms. Have each child glue the gems and sequins of his or her choice onto one or both sides of the CD. It is easiest to start at the center, close to the hole, and move outward. Allow the glue to dry. Then tie string or yarn through the hole. Make sure the string or yarn is long enough for the child to hang the CD from the ceiling or in a window. The gems and sequins catch the light and create sparkles of violet, which is an excellent visualization of the violet flame.

ACTIVITY #3:
Causal-Body Ball

Goal: The goal of this activity is for children to create a three-dimensional representation of the causal body using modeling clay, then slicing it to see the causal body rings.

Materials:

> Modeling clay in the seven colors of the causal body: white, yellow, pink, violet, purple, green, and blue
> Gold glitter
> Seven bowls to hold the clay
> Table knives (not sharp) for cutting the clay causal-body ball later
> Rolling pin
> Chart of Your Divine Self for reference (in this chapter)

Preparation: Put the clay in the seven bowls, one for each color, on a table. Mix a tiny sprinkle of gold glitter into the purple clay to represent the purple and gold band of the causal body. Since the children will be making a causal body in layers, it might help to put the bowls in the order of the colors of the causal body. Set out the table knives, rolling pin, and Chart of Your Divine Self.

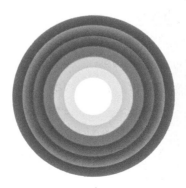

The Activity: Hold up the Chart of Your Divine Self. Explain that they will be making their very own model of a causal body that will be about the size of a grapefruit.

First, have each child make a small white ball of clay at least one inch in diameter. This is the center of the causal body, the I AM Presence. Then, using the Chart of Your Divine Self for reference, add a clay layer in each succeeding color as it appears in the Chart. Around the white ball there will be a yellow layer, then a pink layer, etc., until all the colors of the causal body have been applied, finishing off with the blue layer.

To apply each layer, it might be easiest for the children to make a ball of clay and use the rolling pin to roll it into a flat sheet, about ¼ inch thick. Then they can press this flat piece around the causal-body ball. They can tear off any excess clay so they have the right amount to cover the ball, and then they can press and smooth it down. Bit by bit, they will be building a model of the causal body in all its brilliance! Of course, you can all have fun experimenting with the most effective way to add layers and build your causal-body balls. This will be a unique way for children to understand the three-dimensional nature of their causal bodies, and almost everyone loves to play with clay.

When everyone has completed their layers, they will have clay balls that are about four inches in diameter. Now tell the children that you have something even more exciting for them to do! You can explain that Mark Prophet said that you could cut the causal body in half and see the layers of colors. You can ask them if they would like to do that. They probably will say yes! Give the children table knives and ask them to carefully cut their layered clay ball in half. They should see all the lovely colors in rings, just like the causal body as it appears on the Chart of Your Divine Self—just maybe a tad messier! This might be an "aha" moment for them, and they will always remember the beauty of their causal body.

CHAPTER EIGHT

The Flame in Your Heart

*"Right within this body temple, upon the altar
of the heart, there is burning a flame that is actually
God in manifestation."*

Elizabeth Clare Prophet, *Inner Perspectives*

Love Is the Key to Your Soul's Victory

You feel love for your family, your friends, and your pets. The more love you have, the more you will want to help others. When people are kind and loving to one another, everyone is much happier, don't you think? Have you ever noticed how much better a project goes when you love what you are doing? This might be a project you do with your classmates, or it might be something you make as a special gift for someone. Everything flows so much better when people have love in their hearts. Love makes all the difference. And how do we remove the blocks in order to have more love in our hearts? (You know the answer!) By using the violet flame!

The Divine Spark in Your Heart

The love of our very special friends, the ascended masters, enfolds the entire world. Now that is a lot of love! The love in your heart is God's love right inside of you. How is that possible? Have you ever seen a strawberry plant with long slender runners coming out of it? These little runners grow roots to make brand new strawberry plants. Each new plant is exactly like the parent plant. This is precisely what God has done for each of us. He has given us a tiny part of himself in our heart. This is your divine spark, and it's called your threefold flame. It is God right inside of you. This is big news!

Maybe you're wondering why it's called the threefold flame. "Threefold" means that something has three parts. Therefore the flame in your heart has three parts. Each part, or plume, of the threefold flame is a different color. The blue plume represents the power of God, the yellow plume represents the wisdom of God, and the pink plume represents the love of God. And there it is, right within your very own heart! These three qualities are meant to work together in balance in your life. When you give the violet flame, your threefold flame can spin in perfect balance. Do you have any idea why that would be important?

The Violet Flame Helps Your Threefold Flame Balance and Grow

You may have heard people talk about areas of their life that need to be in balance. They might say it's important to have a balance between work and play. They might say that having a balanced diet is good for your body. Your parents might tell you that you need to have balance between playing with friends and spending time with your family. This concept of balance also works with your beautiful threefold flame. A balanced threefold flame means that all three plumes are the same size. If your threefold flame is balanced, you are probably a wise, loving, and strong person—a well-balanced person. This is a wonderful way to be.

When our souls were first created, we were given a perfectly balanced threefold flame. But over time our threefold flame has become imbalanced through the misuse of energy. This can cause people to be out of sorts. Do you have any thoughts about what it means when people are out of sorts? Well, here are a few examples. A person who misuses the light of the blue plume might be very bossy, but a person who has mastery of the blue plume might be a good leader. A person who misuses the light of the yellow plume might be very brainy and rigid in their thinking, but a person who has mastery of the yellow plume might be very understanding and wise. A person who misuses the light of the pink plume might not like many people, but a person who has mastery of the pink plume may be a loving friend to many.

The violet flame helps get rid of anything that imbalances our threefold flame. When people have a balanced threefold flame, they feel at peace. When the violet flame brings balance to all three plumes of your threefold flame, it makes it possible for your threefold flame to grow. This means you will have more love, wisdom, and power to help you throughout your whole life. What could this mean for you now? Well, your room might be more orderly (power), you might understand the people around you better (wisdom), and you might have lots of wonderful friends (love). When you're older, having these qualities of the threefold flame will help you have a full and meaningful life.

Balancing Your Threefold Flame

It's wonderful to think about the threefold flame in our heart now and then. Here is a violet-flame mantra to help you:

> **Violet fire, thou love divine,**
> **Blaze within this heart of mine!**
> **Thou art mercy forever true,**
> **Keep me always in tune with you.**

Your threefold flame is a gift from God, and you can use the joyful power of the violet flame to help it burn brightly and in perfect balance.

---— **FUN FAMILY ACTIVITIES** —---

ACTIVITY #1:
Spin That Top!

Goal: The purpose of this activity is to show that a balanced top spins much longer and better than an unbalanced top. In the same way, a person with a balanced threefold flame will "spin" through life and accomplish more than a person with an unbalanced threefold flame.

Materials:

    Wooden play tops, one for each child
    Blue, yellow, and pink clay
    A flat surface, such as a wooden floor or concrete slab

Preparation: Collect the materials.

The Activity: Give the children an opportunity to play with the tops and become adept at spinning them. Then give a brief explanation of the threefold flame and its three plumes of blue, yellow, and pink. Briefly explain that the blue plume represents power, the yellow plume represents wisdom, and the pink plume represents love.

Ask each child to pick one color of clay and put a small blob of it on the upper part of the top. Now ask the children to spin their tops again. They will find that the tops wobble and fall over more quickly because they aren't balanced due to the blob of clay. In the same way, our threefold flame doesn't spin as well when it's not balanced. We all can do more with a balanced threefold flame.

ACTIVITY #2:
Threefold-Flame Coloring Sheets

Goal: The goal of this activity is to help children learn about the threefold flame.

Materials:

Threefold-flame coloring sheets, one for each child

https://www.summitlighthouse.org/ThreefoldFlamePage

https://www.summitlighthouse.org/RealSelfColoringPage

Colored pencils, markers, or crayons in blue, yellow, and pink

Preparation: Set up the materials on a table with space for the children to be able to color their sheets comfortably.

The Activity: Let the children color their threefold-flame coloring sheets with the shades of blue, yellow, and pink that appeal to them.

ACTIVITY #3:
Violet-Flame and Threefold-Flame Word Search

Goal: The goal of this activity is to help children become more familiar with the violet flame and their threefold flame by searching for related words.

Materials:
>	Word Search copies
>	Colored pencils, markers, or pens

Preparation: Make the number of Word Search copies you will need for your group.

The Activity: Let the children find the words.

Violet-Flame and Threefold-Flame
Word Search

```
T U C R U L C H I B S S B H J
N R Y M E H C L A A R N O N N
C Z A J O Y F U L L B Q T E E
H V Z N Z N H G J A B K N I P
M C A W S J S P B N G A W G I
S O F R T M E Q F C S S L K C
X Y D V W L U O S E H O A W X
G G W S P B F T P O V H D M X
W Z P R I R A M A E K R C M A
B G U F E W T L R T L N N M O
S P R E B A E P K Y I F A Q B
J J D N P I L W O Z T O K L I
T O O L X M O E Q W R F N B V
M S U S I E I U Y E E I I I E
E T S J T R V Y T K L R X I O
```

Words to search for:

ALCHEMY

POWER

PURPLE

PINK

SPARK

VIOLET

LOVE

TRANSMUTATION

WISDOM

JOYFUL

BALANCE

FREEDOM

FAMILY DEVOTIONS

[To parents:] Children naturally love the violet flame, and they love learning that a simple mantra or prayer can bring the violet flame into their world. They feel the light and freedom that it brings, and it nurtures their inner life and connection with their I AM Presence and Holy Christ Self, their inner teacher.

Family prayer time is very special for children, and what better way to help them learn to pray than praying together as a family. Then when children are older, they will have established the habit of praying and are more likely to establish their own rituals of devotion.

It's exciting for children to have a special place to pray, either when they are alone or when the family prays together. This should be in a quiet area of the home, possibly a corner of the child's room. A simple altar can be created using a small table where the child can place a beautiful cloth, such as a white or violet cloth. If you have a Chart of Your Divine Self that can be used, this would be placed centered along the back of the altar. The child can then place a few of his or her favorite pictures, statues, crystals, etc., on the table so that there are beautiful things to look at while praying. Special times of family devotions can begin in this lovely and peaceful place.

There are different types of prayer. One is the call, or fiat, which we described in chapter one as "Dear God, please send violet flame into this situation now!" Then there is the mantra, which is a very short prayer, such as "I AM a being of violet fire! I AM the purity God desires!" There is another type of prayer that is called a decree, which is a more powerful form of prayer to God. It is a command said in the name of the I AM Presence and Holy Christ Self so that the light Above may become the light below. A decree may be short or long, and it usually starts with a preamble and ends with a closing. All of these forms of prayer are what we call the science of the spoken Word.

The following are a few decrees to the violet flame that the whole family can enjoy doing together. You can use the whole decree or, if your child is too young, you can choose a particular verse that is easier for your child to do.

Please note that the first decree begins with a short preamble and ends with a closing acceptance of what has been invoked. These can be applied to any of the following decrees.

I AM THE VIOLET FLAME

In the name of my beloved I AM Presence and Holy Christ Self, I decree:

I AM the violet flame
In action in me now
I AM the violet flame
To light alone I bow
I AM the violet flame
In mighty cosmic power
I AM the light of God
Shining every hour
I AM the violet flame
Blazing like a sun
I AM God's sacred power
Freeing every one

And in full faith I consciously accept this manifest in full power according to God's will.

RADIANT SPIRAL VIOLET FLAME

Radiant spiral violet flame,
Descend, now blaze through me!
Radiant spiral violet flame,
Set free, set free, set free!

Radiant violet flame, O come,
Expand and blaze thy light through me!
Radiant violet flame, O come,
Reveal God's power for all to see!
Radiant violet flame, O come,
Awake the earth and set it free!

Radiance of the violet flame,
Expand and blaze through me!
Radiance of the violet flame,
Expand for all to see!
Radiance of the violet flame,
Establish mercy's outpost here!
Radiance of the violet flame,
Come, transmute now all fear!

Children Can Have Fun with the Violet Flame

Marching, waltzing, and clapping can make giving violet-flame decrees lots of fun for children. Clapping can also help children learn the right rhythm of a decree.

When you teach violet-flame decrees to children, they can visualize in their mind what is being said in the decree. Children can also march and sing while holding violet-colored pinwheels or pom-poms. Adding such things to decrees makes giving violet-flame decrees a lot more fun!

Through these fun activities, the violet flame can become a song that sings in a child's heart. There is almost no greater gift we can give to our children—and to their future—than the knowledge of the violet flame!

CHAPTER NINE

Nature Spirits—
Our Friends and Helpers

*"There are many kinds of families—our immediate family,
close friends.... We also enjoy our spiritual family—
the ascended masters, the angels and the elementals."*

Elizabeth Clare Prophet, *Pearls of Wisdom,* vol. 41, no. 32

The Violet Flame Helps the Nature Spirits

Many people feel happy when they are outside. Do you feel that way? Walking in a crisp pine forest feels so peaceful. Jumping from stone to stone in the splashing, icy water of a mountain stream is so much fun. Have you ever felt as though you had company when you were outside in the woods, at a lake, or in your garden? Sometimes you can almost catch a glimpse of tiny nature spirits out of the corner of your eye. But when you turn to look, no one is there! Maybe a shy nature spirit was peeking at you!

Gnomes, fairies, and elves are alive and well in cultures around the world. Irish folks believe in little people and leprechauns. Some children have imaginary friends that might just be one of these nature spirits. What is amazing is that these beings are real. They are called elementals, and they love us. In this chapter we will learn more about these friendly beings and how to use the violet flame to help them.

Salamanders, Sylphs, Undines, and Gnomes, Oh My!

Are you a little curious about the different kinds of elementals? Well, there are four kinds. They are called salamanders, sylphs, undines, and gnomes. And these beings don't just sit quietly on spotted mushrooms or float dreamily on puffy clouds! Each kind of elemental has a special job to do in nature. They are very busy! Let's introduce them in more detail now.

Fiery salamanders take care of…surprise…fire! These powerful and loving beings carry dazzling rods of white lightning. Just as a flame flickers and changes, the way fiery salamanders look changes too. Salamanders vary in size—big ones can be nine feet tall, but tiny ones can be only one inch tall!

Next, we have the lovely, airy sylphs. They control the winds and the atmosphere. They create beautiful cloud patterns that look like angels. Mark Prophet explained that the beautiful sylphs have long golden hair and lovely pure faces.

The undines take care of all water. They control the tides, seas, lakes, rivers, and streams. They oversee all precipitation, which is rain, snow, dew, and every form of moisture. They playfully frolic in cool waves and dancing waterfalls. Undines can help us calm our own "water body," which means our emotions. That might be helpful, wouldn't it?

Gnomes are probably the most familiar elementals of all. Gnomes are also called dwarfs or elves. The movie *Snow White and the Seven Dwarfs* gives us a glimpse of what gnomes look like—but they aren't always whistling! Gnomes take care of plants, animals, and minerals. Gnomes were small in the movie, but they can be much larger. Some of the little three-inch-tall gnomes love to play in the grass. Other gnomes are three feet in height. Even bigger gnomes are very tall so that they can take care of the giant redwood trees. Billions of gnomes tend the earth in all four seasons. That's a big job, isn't it?

Gnomes and all the elementals work hard indeed, and they can be helped by the violet flame. Can you imagine how the violet flame might help our dear friends, the elementals?

Elementals Need Violet Flame

Since the elementals take care of the earth, they also help bear the weight of the misuse of mankind's energy. For example, this misuse of energy can cause pollution around the cities. They feel the weight of this energy, sometimes just as if they were carrying it on their backs. Sometimes this energy gets very difficult for them to carry. We can also think of this as carrying mankind's karma. When people aren't taking good care of the earth or they're not handling their own energy very well, it makes the elementals sad. This karma upon the elementals can cause hurricanes, tornados, and all kinds of storms and natural disasters because they can only carry so much.

When we help the elementals by sending lots of violet flame their way, it takes away the burdens they carry. Sometimes sending them lots of violet flame can even prevent big storms or other natural disasters from happening. It can also help our trees, water, air, and land, and then the entire world can become cleaner, lighter, and more beautiful. Isn't it wonderful that we have the violet flame to help the elementals?

When the violet flame clears the elementals of the weight of karma, it makes them feel light and joyful again! And guess what? In addition to doing violet flame to lighten their loads, you can ask them to decree along with you. That's right! The elementals love to decree! They need to decree with you because they don't have their own threefold flame, and neither do animals. But the elementals and animals can earn a threefold flame through their loving service to mankind. If you invite the elementals to decree with you, they will follow your example because they adore the threefold flame. And this will help them earn their own!

You can even invite a whole troop of elementals to join you as you pray, sing, and decree. Elementals will jump with joy to join you at your altar. You could even have little cushions for them to sit on! Figurines of gnomes and other nature spirits placed on your altar will surely make them smile too. It's so much fun to have elementals around! Here is a little violet-flame mantra you can give for the elementals any time:

The elementals are beings of violet fire!
The elementals are the purity God desires!

The Elementals Want to Help Us!

The elementals are just waiting for us to ask for their help. The ascended masters have told us that we each have twelve elementals given to us. Imagine that! You have your very own troop of nature spirits to help you with all kinds of things! For example, if you can't find your backpack or your soccer shoes and you need them right away, you can ask your twelve elementals to help you find them! Or if you're waiting for a friend to call you and you've been waiting a very long time, you can ask your elementals to tap your friend on the shoulder to remind him or her to call you. You can also ask your elementals to do a specific job by a certain time.

When you call to your twelve elementals, these new friends will be helping you, playing with you, and decreeing with you each day. Again, just like asking for the violet flame to come into your world, all you have to do to invite the elementals to be with you and to help you is to simply ask. You can say something like, "My beloved elementals, please help me with [_____]," and they will very happily come!

FUN FAMILY ACTIVITIES

ACTIVITY #1:
Making Outdoor Elemental Homes

Goal: The goal of this activity is to create lovely places in your yard or garden for the elementals to live and play in.

Materials:
    Sticks, grass, rocks
    Small figurines of gnomes, fairies, or other nature spirits

Preparation: Let children gather their materials.

The Activity: Children can use their imaginations to create special places for the elementals.

ACTIVITY #2:
Make an Elemental Diorama

Goal: This is a fun activity to help children feel closer to the elementals.

Materials:
>A small box, such as a shoebox
>Objects from nature, such as pebbles, stones, twigs, flowers, and grass
>Glue

Preparation: Have the children decide what kind of elementals will live and play in their diorama.

The Activity: Children can collect materials and create a home for their elementals, depending on the kind of elemental they choose. For example, for an undine they might want to have pictures of waterfalls or streams. Children might get very creative and have all kinds of ideas, such as adding a hammock, swimming pool, a little house, and more.

ACTIVITY #3:
Family Violet-Flame Gardens

Goal: This activity will provide a practical way for the whole family to celebrate the violet flame. Find a good spot in your yard and plant a violet-flame garden made up of violet, purple, and pink flowers. If you don't have a good place in your yard or you live in an apartment, you can make your garden in a wooden box or planter that can hang from your window. You can also plant your garden in a bigger wooden box to put on your porch. Or, if you would like to have an indoor garden, you might consider an African violet plant.

Materials:

Seeds or flowers of various shades of violet, purple, and pink

Garden tools, such as a shovel and a spade

Garden gloves, if desired

Fertilizer

Watering can

Preparation: Collect your seeds or flowers and gather your tools. Select a spot for your garden.

The Activity: As a family, design and plant your garden. Each family member can help maintain the garden by watering, weeding, and fertilizing it. You can ask the elementals to help you, and you can even talk to your flowers. You can also give violet-flame decrees for your flowers.

Please see the following links for fun coloring sheets on the elementals.

https://www.summitlighthouse.org/GirlGnome
https://www.summitlighthouse.org/BoyGnome
https://www.summitlighthouse.org/VioletFlameColoringPage

CHAPTER TEN

Let the Violet Flame Sparkle and Shine around the World!

"A million or ten million people invoking the violet flame could, according to God's mercy, turn back the karma earth's evolutions have created...."

Elizabeth Clare Prophet, *The Astrology of the Four Horsemen*

People Pray in Their Own Way All Over the World

Every day, all around the world, people of different faiths reach up to God. Buddhists calmly meditate as wisps of incense fill the air. They hang their bright prayer flags out in the gentle wind. Christians pray fervently on their knees. They ignite golden candle flames in dark, peaceful churches. Hindus joyously give their devotion through songs called bhajans. They sing, dance, and count their prayer beads. Muslims unroll their beautiful prayer rugs. They reverently bow to the holy city of Mecca five times a day. All of this devotion reaches God's heart.

Why do people pray? Devoted people ask for God's help for themselves, their families, and their communities. In this book you have been learning about a unique way to reach up to God, and that is by invoking the sparkling, bubbling, joyful violet flame.

All ways of reaching up to God are important, but now you know a little more about why Saint Germain's gift of the violet flame is extraordinary. Did you know that there is something even more far-reaching that you can do with the violet flame?

The Violet Flame Helps World Situations

You have probably thought about situations at your school that might need some violet flame. You may have also thought about friends who might be having trouble in a certain class or friends who are having trouble with each other. Those situations could use a burst of violet flame to help them! You can also expand the circle of violet flame to your town. Do people drop trash in the park? Maybe you can send those people some violet flame so they will pick up trash instead of leaving it everywhere. Serious problems, like crime and violence, can also be saturated, uplifted and changed by the violet flame. The violet flame can do much more too—far beyond your school and town. (But remember, change can take time.)

Have you ever seen something on the news that made you feel like you just had to do something to help, but you didn't know what to do? Maybe it was a problem halfway around the world. Well, here is some good news: The violet flame will travel right from your heart and through your spoken decrees directly to that situation. The violet-flame decrees that you give can be sent to specific parts of the world where people are having challenges. Through the power of the spoken Word you can send this intense light of freedom to places where people are suffering. You can send the violet flame into war, famine, poverty, and all kinds of situations. Sometimes it's helpful to read a newspaper or watch the news to know what to pray for. The violet flame can bring change, freedom from suffering, and resolution to difficult problems anywhere on earth.

Give Decrees with Your Whole Heart

Remember, if you put your whole heart into something, whatever you try to accomplish works out better. This is also true with decrees. When you put your whole heart into saying your violet-flame decrees, they will work better too. You might even feel like your heart is warmer as you decree and as you send light into personal or world situations. It might be comforting for you to know that many saints in centuries past have had that very same feeling! It can be a sign that your decrees and prayers are working because you are doing them from your whole heart. But if you don't feel it, that's ok too. This light in your heart makes a huge difference. Did you know that there is a special word for people who carry this light of God in their hearts?

Lightbearers around the World

As we have mentioned in the beginning of this chapter, people all over the world pray for the light of God to help them. We are all connected by this same light, even if we belong to separate churches and have different beliefs. There is a wonderful word for people who carry this light. This very special word is *lightbearer*. There are lightbearers all over the world in various countries who have different and unique traditions and cultures. But the light in the heart of every lightbearer is the same, even if the color of their skin is not! We may not speak the same language, but the language of the heart is universal.

As lightbearers, we hold light within our heart that helps others in the world. This is what the violet flame can help you do. You can hold greater light and share it with others. That is what being a lightbearer is all about. You have friends all over the world you haven't met, but you share the same light of God that is within them. Have you ever met someone you clicked with right away? That is what lightbearers often feel when they first meet. Lightbearers can unite through loving and expanding the beautiful flame of freedom, the violet flame.

Moving Forward in the Light of Freedom

Oh my! Are you feeling a little saturated right now with all you've learned about the violet flame? That's OK! You can let it soak in over time. You can think about what you want to do with this amazing gift of freedom from the heart of Saint Germain. He is ready and waiting to help you. You can discover the changes that can come to you and others by using the violet flame. This wonderful gift from Saint Germain will help the whole world come into the golden age of Aquarius. Have you ever heard of the Aquarian age before?

The Aquarian age is a new era when the winds of freedom bring light and creativity to all areas of life. People will create inventions that change the world. They will find more peace within as they become closer to God. They will discover their real purpose. The Aquarian age will bring the light of freedom to all parts of the world. You can help this happen, both in your own life and in the lives of those around you, simply by using the violet flame. What an amazing opportunity!

"Give your calls to the violet flame!
Do not fail to do it!
For the violet flame is your safety belt.
That's what it's all about."

Beloved Jesus, *Pearls of Wisdom*, vol. 39, no. 42

FUN FAMILY ACTIVITIES

ACTIVITY #1:
Violet Flame around the Globe

Goal: The goal of this activity is to send violet flame into specific areas of the world.

Materials:
A globe, or a map of the world if a globe isn't available

Preparation: Collect your globe or map and place it on a table or central area where people can gather around it. It is also helpful to read the newspaper or watch the news to know about specific problems in different areas of the world, depending on the ages of your children. It might be helpful to have everyone write down details about the problems that need the violet flame.

The Activity: Explain that everyone will be sending violet flame into areas of the world that are burdened with problems. Ask everyone to invite their troop of elementals to join all of you in invoking the violet flame! Then, using the globe or map, hold your hands over the problem area and visualize the violet flame going from your heart and through your hands right into that geographic location. As you give violet-flame mantras and decrees, imagine the violet flame penetrating deeper and deeper into the area, clearing all problems and burdens at that location.

ACTIVITY #2:
Miracle Pouch Family Fun

Goal: The goal of this activity is for children to make their own miracle pouch.

Saint Germain said: *"I give to you a pouch, a purse of miracle joy. It is yours to take. It is yours to enjoy. This great miracle sense, this sphere of love that I hurl, is for you to carry and to take out of your briefcase or whatever it is that you carry for the most precious of your treasures from day to day. For here and there, when you come upon those situations that only the miracle alchemy of Saint Germain will dissolve, then you can take out this precious miracle light. It is an energy from my heart."*

Saint Germain, *Pearls of Wisdom,* vol. 59, no. 1

Materials: You can find instructions on the Internet for many types of pouches with varying degrees of difficulty. Choose one that best fits the ages and interest of your children.

A purple or violet cloth

Scissors, needle, and thread

Shiny violet paper to put into the pouch

Any other materials you might want to add as decorations to the pouch

Preparation: Gather the materials and place them on a large table or other work area.

The Activity: Make the pouches. Then, as a family, you can toss your pouches to each other and visualize them going into family, community, or world issues as you say the miracle pouch mantra. You can fill in the blank with anything you want, such as "the problem on my bus route," "the crime in my town," "the hurricane in Texas," "the war in Afghanistan." Each person has an opportunity to choose where to hurl the miracle pouch. It can be a personal or a world situation.

Saint Germain, hurl your miracle pouch into [_____].

ACTIVITY #3:
Keep a Violet-Flame Recording-Angel Journal

Goal: The goal of this activity is to help keep track of how the violet flame is working for you.

Materials:

A notebook or bound journal

A pen or pencil, maybe a violet-colored one just for fun!

Preparation: Collect the materials and have your journal close by.

The Activity: Did you know that special angels keep track of everything that happens on earth? They are called recording angels. You can be a recording angel too. Try giving some violet-flame mantras about a situation with your friends, your family, your school, or anything else you like. Write a sentence (or more) each day to record what is happening as you send some violet flame into that situation. See what happens with the miracle light of the violet flame!

EPILOGUE

With the compassion and transforming quality of the violet flame, Elizabeth Clare Prophet delivers the following violet-flame meditation. Together, you and your children can bask in the comforting essence of this miraculous light as you give this meditation time and time again.

**Devotions: Violet Flame Crystal Meditation
led by Elizabeth Clare Prophet**
https://www.youtube.com/
watch?v=3mVOKzv2eYQ&list=PL16B4CB58B3F19AA2&index=10

Be Empowered!
Be Inspired!

As you experience the blessings and challenges of family life, gaining a spiritual perspective can be very empowering.

To continue learning more about the stupendous violet flame and to enhance your family's spirituality, connect with us! Access more practical tools and inspiring resources to assist you.

- Cutting-edge articles for parents
  https://www.summitlighthouse.org/Parenting

- Spiritual lessons for children
  https://www.summitlighthouse.org/ChildrenSpiritualLessons

- Principles of Montessori education
  https://www.summitlighthouse.org/MontessoriEducation

- Much more

  You can also learn more about the violet flame at
  https://www.summitlighthouse.org/VioletFlameResources

VIOLET FLAME: *Alchemy for Personal Change*
by Elizabeth Clare Prophet

Learn how to use a high-frequency spiritual energy to transform your life and the world around you!

Ongoing scientific advances and studies point to what sages knew thousands of years ago: sound holds the key to the mysteries of the universe. Mystical traditions East and West embrace the concept of a spiritual fire. Elizabeth Clare Prophet's new book on the violet flame will show that sound, in the form of mantras, prayers, decrees and affirmations, can be used to call forth a spiritual fire known as the violet flame to transform every aspect of our lives and change our spiritual destinies.

Mrs. Prophet shares how we can harness the power of the violet flame by applying practical spiritual techniques to help restore health, balance, harmony as well as aide in creating positive and lasting changes to our personal lives, the lives of our loved ones and to the world around us.

VIOLET FLAME: *To Heal Body, Mind and Soul*
by Elizabeth Clare Prophet

This pocket guide describes how to use a high-frequency, spiritual energy to increase vitality, overcome blocks to healing, dissolve records of trauma and create positive change in our personal lives and for the planet. Learn how the violet flame can be used to increase vitality and to assist any healing process of the body, mind, emotions or spirit.

Includes: Inspiring true stories and nine easy steps to begin using the violet flame with affirmations, mantras, and visualizations.

The Summit Lighthouse®
63 Summit Way
Gardiner, Montana 59030 USA

1-800-245-5445 / 406-848-9500

Se habla espanol.

TSLinfo@TSL.org
SummitLighthouse.org

Mark L. Prophet (1918–1973) and Elizabeth Clare Prophet (1939–2009), were visionary pioneers of modern spirituality and internationally renowned authors. Their books are published in more than 30 languages, and millions of copies have been sold online and in bookstores worldwide.

Together, they built a worldwide spiritual organization that is helping thousands to find their way out of human problems and reconnect to their inner divinity. They walked the path of spiritual adeptship, advancing through the universal initiations common to mystics of both East and West. They taught about this path and described their own experiences for the benefit of all who desire to make spiritual progress.

Mark and Elizabeth left an extensive library of spiritual teachings from the ascended masters and a thriving, worldwide community of people who study and practice these teachings.